A DIVINE JOURNEY

DENNIS A. MCINTYRE

BENNETT
MEDIA & MARKETING

A DIVINE JOURNEY

Bennett books may be ordered through booksellers or by contacting:

Bennett Media and Marketing
1603 Capitol Ave., Suite 310 A233
Cheyenne, WY 82001
www.thebennettmediaandmarketing.com
Phone: 1-307-202-9292

ISBN: 978-1-957114-38-5 (Paperback)
ISBN: 978-1-957114-39-2 (eBook)

Printed in the United States of America

Bennett Media rev. date: 04/08/2022

FOREWORD

"The Quilt" is published about our family and how God has been blessing us through several generations. I commend my older brother, David, for researching our history beginning with our father's military campaigns. God was watching over our dad, while bullets flew all around. The book continues to show how a blanket of protection was on our entire family over decades. That work triggered thoughts about my life travels.

My journey led me to recall significant events where God was in control of many twists and turns. From high school through adulthood, significant decisions have to be made. Some of these include my career path, wife, fatherhood, and retirement. Little did I realize that the direction taken was the result of following God's leading. It was only as I look back that I can see those situations and events that shaped my life and continues to do so even now. It is my hope that my story will cause readers to reflect similar events in their lives and praise God for his care. We are not here alone. That much I have learned is true.

All of us face decisions daily. Sometimes, we might wish for a crystal ball to see the results of our choices in advance and avoid the wrong ones. Knowing that God was in control in my life makes all the difference. The Bible is a complete love letter to His creation. It covers events of the past through the future. It is our crystal ball if we read it and accept God's promise that He will not leave us or forsake us.

Matthew 28: 20b (NIV)

"lo, I am with you always, even unto the end of the world. A'-men."

Genesis defines God's creation. Revelation defines a new heaven and earth, written a few thousand years later. The eternal God is in control of everything, yet desires only the best for us. Take this journey with me to see His handiwork and give thanks as I hope you see that work in your life as well.

CONTENTS

Dennis A. McIntyre

Introduction

Life is a journey full of twists, turns, and unexpected events. The older I get, the faster time seems to travel. As I reflect on where my journey has taken me, one thing is certain, namely, I am not alone. Some may think that we are here by pure chance as reflected in the school textbooks. For me, there are far too many events, or circumstances that speak volumes to the contrary. To those who believe those things are just coincidences, I hope to offer evidence that may change their minds.

After losing my wife in 2007, writing became a coping mechanism. In 2011 a friend asked me to write a man's story. He had a completely changed life from one of destruction, crime and hopelessness to joy. My first novel, "Shackled Yet Free" was the result. The man's name was changed to Jake. It was self-published so that copies could be readily obtained for my friend and Jake's family. I never thought of myself as a novelist, but that was the approach that I took to writing his story. Though most of the work was true, based on the interview, the ending was fictionalized in an attempt to add closure. To my surprise, several readers from my local church commented on looking forward to the next book. His journey had taken him through dark times until God took over. He was completely changed.

Somehow, the reader's comments inspired me to write two more books, taking Jake's life to new frontiers. I had no idea where each story would lead, but I accepted the challenge. "Freedom's Journey" and "Free to Serve" quickly followed to appease them. Each night I had a place to go to escape from the loneliness of living alone. Each morning I was amazed to read the words that I wrote. It was as if someone else had pressed the keys on my keyboard.

Eleven years later I felt led to republish all three books. To do so meant that I would have to read, edit, and format them. This process left me feeling somewhat awestruck by the words I had written over a decade earlier. I could not believe that I actually wrote novels. More than that, as I reread each one, I could not remember where the next chapter would lead. It was as if the words were placed there without my knowledge. I remember typing each night for less than a month for both books.

Each morning I would read the previous night's work with the thought; "Did I write that?" Yet, the next chapter would flow. Recently, a professional reader gave a five star review of both works, through a publishing agent. The reviews prompted a response to write once again.

This is my journey. I pray that my readers will get a sense of joy and recognize that they are not alone in this thing called life.

Early Years

When we think about going on a journey, the beginning may be the best place to start. Often, we enter a new frontier with heavy preparation, like school, vacations, marriage, and more. Anticipation is as much a part of the trip, which may trigger many questions like:

…Am I ready?

…Do I have everything I need?

…Am I making the right choices?

…What can I expect when I get there?

…More

These are not present when we are born into this world. Parents, caregivers, friends, family, and other intangibles mold our lives. It is only when we look back that we can sense how we had been prepared for the journey of life. Looking back, however, provides insights for us to consider.

I do not remember anything prior to the age of three or four. I never knew my mother who died when I was three. The first memory I have is not a good one. I was the middle of three brothers who spent five years together in foster homes. Our father would visit occasionally, but the family we knew was not our own.

Life may have dealt others a bad hand, but I hope that my journey will be a source of encouragement to my readers. Questions permeated my thoughts for a long time. "Why did my mother have to die?" "Doesn't anybody love me?" That question, in particular, seemed to mold my early childhood. Watching home movies helped to bring light to why I felt that way. I am confident that my parents loved me by their interaction, but early foster home care told a different story.

Not all foster homes were difficult. The last one was the longest and by far the best. A farmer and his wife took three boys in, despite a large family of their own. We were loved and appreciated by everyone. My older brother grew especially close to them. We had our chores to do around the farm along with dishwashing, drying, and other things, but that made us feel as part of a family. Every Sunday we would go to church and enjoy a large dinner together. That was a welcomed time.

Dad remarried and we became a new family unit when I was eight or nine. Life was not going to be a cakewalk, but we were together. That offered hope. The early years are considered formative. They shape our emotional states, our thought processes, and other traits. The roads we travel later in life will have obstacles and decisions that further develop our character. A person going through tough times, like the loss of a loved one, can become an encourager for someone going through similar things in the present. That is my conclusion today.

Pastors have told me that I have the gift of encouragement, but I used to deny it. My early life in those foster homes was discouraging, so I should be the one who needs to be encouraged. At least that was my thought. After the loss of my wife, I published my first book titled: "Legacy of Love." I originally wrote it as a legacy about my father, spiral bound it, and gave it to family members. Others would read it and tell me to get it published, but I refused. After all, it was about my dad. Why would strangers read it? More about this will come later.

Ephesians 2:10(KJV):

"For we are his workmanship, created in Christ Jesus unto good works, which God hath before ordained that we should walk in them."

Those words struck me like the proverbial two-by-four. I read them many times before, but they came to life during my wife's battle with cancer. Knowing that God had a plan for my life from inception brought great peace during a tough time. Watching changed lives was even more evidence. Those words brought new insights for my entire life, even my childhood. The why questions were answered. I have a purpose *"in Christ Jesus unto good works,"* which defines me as I journey on.

The time spent in the last foster home introduced me to the knowledge that God exists, but that was only at a surface level. Each meal began with prayer and we attended a church on Sunday. Once we were united as a new family, those things stopped. When I became a father, faith became too important to ignore. Unfortunately, that has changed in our culture. Affluence, two parents working, and the removal of God from classrooms has taken a toll. Money, power, and success are now gods for so many. Those things are not bad in themselves, but having a personal relationship with my spiritual father outweighs them all.

TEEN YEARS

T he transitional years prior to adulthood offered directional changes in human life. The high school we attended was about two miles away, which my brothers and I usually walked. We lived in a valley with several farms, which were a source of income for me to earn. Math and science courses filled my school classes, which came easy for all my brothers as well. Completing homework in class freed up my evenings to work on the farms. Dad's meager income meant that we would not enjoy some luxuries as our schoolmates, but life was good. The extra income allowed for me to save for my first car, buy fuel and other items.

Farm work was welcomed, though often hard. The knowledge learned helped me tremendously in my career path, which will be introduced later. When things broke on the farm, creativity often resulted in less costly repairs, a lesson that my career path used frequently. Living on a farm, during those foster years, provided firsthand knowledge as well.

My older brother used his high school years academically to score high on his SAT tests and earn college tuition. He completed schoolwork at home, while my books hit the bed and I would head out to the farms. My younger brother spent the time with friends without sacrificing good grades. Report cards were never a problem, as far as our parents were concerned. Dad lost his father prior to high school and had to quit to help his mother on the farm. So each report card was received with pride. Being together as a family meant that we desired to please our parents.

That was not the case between brothers, however. Occasional B grades were fine for me, but unacceptable for my older brother. Special recognition should have been given to him, but it was not. Saving money to buy my first car was one goal. Passing my driver's test on it a week or two later added some jealousy. Though each brother took different paths in life, we all came to similar places, which will also be covered later. Our math and science skills were passed down from our biological mother and served us well.

Our teen years helped to prepare us for what lied ahead. Although we were academically skilled, none of us were heavy in sports. On those days when farm work was not available, I might be seen pitching horseshoes with my dad in the yard. Stakes were placed forty feet apart between sickle pear trees. Dad had won local championships pitching shoes and maintained his practice in the yard. He would spot me fifteen points in a game to twenty-one and I only remember winning one time. I remember tossing five ringers in a row, only to have him throw six. Yet, spending time with him was very special. On another occasion, he placed a small sickle pear at the base of a stake. Then he threw a ringer on his first attempt without touching the pear. It was truly amazing.

Dad enjoyed planting a garden as well. Vegetables were a necessary part of our diet. Fresh vegetables were especially welcomed. When dad hoed or watered, I felt the urge to help. Spending time with him was not only enjoyable, but it may have filled a void in my heart caused by the foster home separation. On another occasion, dad was cementing flat stones on a patio between the house and a detached garage. The work was hard on the knees, but I would help gather and wash the stones to help him. He did not have to get up from the patio until finished for the night, so the work may have been less stressful for him. At any rate we bonded.

Dad also enjoyed darts and card playing. He was a life master at the bridge tables. I would play darts with him in a game called "301." The game starts with a double or bulls-eye and ends in like manner. Each time points are scored; the amount is deducted starting with 301. The final double must reach zero exactly to complete the game. Dad would hit the initial double and get down to the final double quickly, while I struggled to hit the first one. I think he enjoyed the game until I would finally score, get to the last double shot and hit it on the first attempt. That would happen frequently, although he might call it luck. Anytime the board was available, he was up to a new challenge. The competition was great, but spending time together was even better.

I also played gin rummy, bridge and a game called euchre. The first two were with dad, while euchre was a game designed, ideally, for four players. Dad taught us and welcomed each game. He didn't tolerate bad play very well, especially, when introduced to a novice bridge player in match play. Poor play would place that person on a "don't call again" list, except with me. If I made a mistake, dad would gently let me know how I should have played. Taking an interest in the things he enjoyed was special. Card playing together carried through our adult life.

Many of these activities were taken from dad after a stroke. He remembered doing them, but playing a game like gin rummy was no longer possible. Dad would hold the cards, but did not know what to do with them. Even that was part of God's plan, as we will see later.

FAMILY VACATIONS

V acation times added to the journey in a big way. The most notable trips during our early years involved fishing in upstate New York's Thousand Islands. With finances low, fishing was the first and usually only option. In preparation for each trip, dad would give us a penny per night crawler, which we would collect by flashlight at a freshly watered golf course. Often, we would stay out until we earned a dollar apiece, which could be used to buy treats on vacation. Dad would carefully prepare a large box with layers of wet newspapers between dozens of worms. The bait would last our entire trip.

Each trip involved a challenge for who would catch the biggest fish, a contest that dad loved to win. Untangling fishing lines by three novice fishermen may have seemed frustrating, but spending time with his sons outweighed the tasks. Frying fish each night for dinner added a fitting closure to each day.

Driving for four hours with the family offered additional challenges. To counter the "Are we there yet?" questions, dad would introduce us to road games. One game involved horses and graveyards. Each time we saw a horse, we would yell out "Horses." The first to yell would get the number of horses viewed added to their account. White ones were counted double. Upon seeing a graveyard, we would yell, "Bury 'Em." The first to yell would keep their horses and the others would be buried (totals go to zero). The winner was the one who had the most horses at the end of the trip. Dad always won, because he knew where the graveyards were and yelled first. Still, it was a time to remember and made the trip enjoyable. I think God may have smiled at the interaction.

My brothers and I were between the ages of nine to eleven on one vacation. We had butch haircuts, which dad gave us prior to the vacation. I remember fishing with my brothers on the dock near the cabin where we stayed. I must have thought that I needed to cast further out to catch the biggest fish. Anyway, the next thing I remember was looking at fish swimming under the water. Then I felt my head being pulled out of the water. Our new mom, Lena, heard the splash and ran to pull me out by grabbing my short hair. I don't think I made the same casting mistake after that. Looking back, however, tells me that God was watching. I could have drowned as I had not learned how to swim and we would go fishing without anyone there to watch over us. Yet, Lena was there.

Fishing with dad was a tradition that was maintained long into our adult life. A quarter was placed on the biggest fish and dad still enjoyed collecting it, despite the moneys spent for bait and tackle. My older brother, David, enjoyed fishing as his main pastime and would welcome dad's visits to join him on the Florida Keys.. The boat trip, several miles out on the ocean, would create seasickness on most occasions, but dad still wanted to spend the time with his son. He was especially happy when I would join them. After all, it meant another quarter in bragging rights.

David enjoyed singing, writing songs, and playing the guitar. We enjoyed listening. After our stepmom passed away, we decided to gather families together on a vacation in a cabin in the mountains of North Carolina. The cabin slept twelve or more. My family of four, David's family of five, my daughter's boyfriend, my son's girlfriend, her daughter and dad were present. On the first night, we started a small bonfire to roast marshmallows and gather around to sing as the guitar played. The next evenings were repeated in like manner, except dad went early to prepare the fire, gather wood, etc. It was special to him and even more to us. Perhaps, God enjoyed our fellowship as well.

Vacations as a family while we were young were a welcomed break from the everyday challenges. School, dad working and other events severely limited the time we spent together. Scheduling vacations with our individual families in later years was necessary. David and I would get together in the Carolinas often with our new families. Our children looked forward to each occasion as much as we did. Our wives were best friends before we knew them, so that added to the excitement. The memories from those trips are still talked about when we get together.

We need rest from the everyday stresses. Rests calm and rejuvenate us. We become more productive in our workplaces, better parents, and more joyful. It is hard for me to picture a journey without those times of recuperation. God rested after completing his creation, an example for us as well.

Genesis 2:1-2 (KJV)

"THUS the heavens and the earth were finished, and all the host of them.

And on the seventh day God ended his work which he had made; and he rested on the seventh day from all his work which he had made."

YOUNG ADULTHOOD

The next major transition in life comes when we finish high school and take the next step. For some, like my brothers, involved college. That was not my desire for many reasons. First, I enjoyed working with my hands. I could learn more from doing than from books and lectures. Second, I knew that my parents could not afford college and I didn't want to burden them. Third, I did not know what I wanted to do as a career vocation. I think that the third reason was the most convincing.

I enjoyed living in my parent's house, so that was not in the equation. I had a car and paid for gas, insurance and maintenance without help from dad. Dad's boss owned a series of apartment buildings and hired me to help maintain them. The $1.75 per hour wage was almost double what I could make on the farms. My work, however, utilized many of the skills that I learned there. The hours fell within my dad's schedule so we could share rides together.

A large corporation, which I won't name, had better opportunities and I applied. I knew that working on apartments was not a career path. The pay was higher in the corporation and overtime was even better. After working there for about ten months, I received my draft notice. I don't remember how high my number was, but I remember wanting to serve in a way that would use my skills. I went down to the local draft board to take a skills test and passed with top scores. That allowed me to choose a career path in electronics in the United States Air Force. Dad was a WWII veteran with heavy combat experience. My older brother enlisted in the Navy reserve while in college followed with two years active duty. My younger brother was drafted in the army after completing four years of college.

I received nine months of technical training in Chanute, Illinois as an autopilot specialist. I worked on B52 bombers and C135 cargo refueling planes. The world of transistors was in its infant stage which would replace the vacuum tubes used in the 1960's. The work was rewarding. I was applying classroom knowledge to hands-on experience and thoroughly enjoyed it. I am still amazed to know that these planes are still used today, although the technology is much improved.

During the technical training in Illinois, I started dating a beautiful young lady in a college town about fifteen miles from the base. I had a car on base and spent many hours with her on weekends. I thought she would be the one that I would have a family with, so the relationship continued for months after being transferred to a SAC base in Michigan about nine or ten hours away by car. Then my hopes were dashed. I made the long drive only to find her with another airman. I ran into a ditch driving back about seven hours later. I was turned off with dating. That was around Thanksgiving of 1967.

I invited a local airman, whom I will call Bob, to come home with me the following Christmas and he agreed. The drive would take us across Canada for a five-hundred-mile trip. The last thing I wanted was a woman in my life, but God had other plans. My older brother and his girlfriend offered to double date with Bob and I. His girlfriend had a roommate and close friend named Dottie. She would join us to go bowling, so off we went.

That seemed okay to me. Bob could be Dottie's date, leaving me the odd man out. After all, I had no interest in dating, or so I thought. Dottie was five foot two, blue eyes, and very pleasing to my eye. Before the night was over, my heart was smitten. Bob did not show any romantic interest in her, allowing me to make a move. After bowling, we dropped Bob off at our parent's house and we spent the rest of the evening with the girls. I found out later, that Bob had a girlfriend near the base and married her soon after.

That was a defining moment for me. God chose Dottie to be my helpmate. Before the trip was over, I told her that if she were to travel to the base in Michigan, I would have a gift for her. She knew that I meant an engagement ring. I was sure that she was to be my wife and lifelong companion. I could not explain it, but another chapter in my life was being written. A few months later the girls made the trip and the rest is history.

We were married on August seventeenth nineteen hundred and sixty-eight. The weeks and months in between were filled with hundred-dollar phone bills and long letters, especially during the twelve-hour charge of quarter's duties in the barracks. A roll of brown wrapping paper about three feet wide was often used for writing material. Dottie learned a great deal about things happening in the barracks, what TV shows were on, and more, as the brown paper was six, eight or ten feet long with small script. She could use them for window shades.

On one occasion, I cut a three-foot circle out of the paper and began writing from the outside edge towards the middle. Dottie took forever to read it, as the words seemed to run together. She countered with a typewritten letter on toilet paper for me. The drive to see her on long weekends or extended leaves seemed like minutes compared to the trip back. Often, Dottie would bake brownies for me to enjoy on the base, but they would not make it the entire trip. Her pet phrase involved jumping on her "Mini Jet" to be with me. She may have thought she was Wonder Woman, but she was my wonder.

After a honeymoon in the Pocono Mountains of Pennsylvania, we began our married life in a rental outside the base. A week later, I was sent to Goose Bay, Labrador for an assignment for six weeks. Dottie had to manage life without me in a new location. She would receive my full pay while I received an additional dollar a day extra for the duty. Phone calls and letters were once again in the offering.

When the assignment was over, I was confronted with the news that we had to move out of the rental. Rodents were a problem. We moved into a one-bedroom cabin closer to the base. Each cabin had similar Air Force couples, and our life together began anew. The cabin was about twenty-feet square (400 sq. feet), with a bedroom, a living room, a small dining space, a tight bathroom, and a narrow kitchen. We never thought it was too small, but rather that it was cozy.

To supplement our income, Dottie worked in a finance office nearby. It was similar to the same work she did in New York State. We were able to purchase our first new car, a 1969 Oldsmobile Cutlass. Then I received orders to go to Thailand. Dottie decided to quit her job and move back home near her parents, rather than spend a year alone near the base. The orders were later cancelled and everything changed. Up to that point we decided to delay having children. With her job gone, she felt ready. Birth control was stopped and our life would be blessed with our son, Jeffery, born on the base. I believe God had those details worked out as well.

Less than five months later, I would leave the Air Force and begin life back in New York. The company, that employed me prior to my enlistment, guaranteed a job when I returned without any loss in seniority. That may have been the deciding factor for not reenlisting. The transition would be smooth as the Air Force took care of the moving expenses. We were able to rent the lower half of a small Cape Cod style house that was owned by Dottie's previous landlord two years earlier.

Although I had a job waiting, I was told to wait three weeks before starting. I worked ten months prior to leaving and now had four years and ten months seniority. The company credited service time as if I was still employed. That meant that I had three weeks' vacation coming before the end of the year. Since it was now near the end of the year, the company did not want me to begin training for the new position and then leave on vacation. That was tremendous as we could get settled without the interruption of going to work. I believe God had prepared every detail. The best part was that an additional three weeks' vacation was available in the next year.

The work was good, but not in my career path. The Air Force taught me electronics. Now I worked the late-night shift in shipping and receiving, totally unrelated to my desired career.. Then another door opened. The company decided to open up several apprenticeships for employees to apply. I jumped on the electrical option and was accepted. That would be a three-year period with each graduate assigned the title of electrician. Pay would be higher, overtime was expected, and my hours would change to the normal dayshift. The GI bill allowed me to receive additional benefits. God was moving quickly.

The owner of the house that we rented refused to make necessary repairs. That initiated a desire to move and our first house became a reality. It was located within walking distance of my work. Although it was only two bedrooms, it felt bigger. God was moving again.

The apprenticeship took on a new twist. Typically, the training was on the job with other electricians, but the company felt led to prepare graduates for more challenging needs in the future. We would spend one day a week in a classroom taking college courses and get paid for it. The instructor was a older company man who received the textbooks from a local college, the Rochester Institute of Technology (RIT). To instruct meant that he had to learn the material, make a class agenda and then lead the class. The courses included algebra, geometry, and calculus, which fit my background perfectly. Often the instructor would call on me to lead the class. At the end of the three-year timeframe, each student could pay small fees to challenge each course and obtain one third of a two-year technical degree. A graduate of the apprenticeship would earn a higher pay grade as an electrical technician.

This allowed time for additional classes in the evening to add to the degree completion. My Air Force training and strong background in the math and science arenas gave me an easier road to travel. Only one other student completed all classes to receive the technician rating. Apprenticeships like that were halted afterwards. Perhaps, the company felt that it was a failure with only two people completing all of the courses, but it was a huge break for me. God opened a door for the college training that I needed.

Shortly after completing the program, my wife and I were expecting a new member of our family, a girl named Tricia. Now the two-bedroom house was in dire need of expansion. Without contacting a realtor, I was approached by the other program graduate with an offer to purchase our home. He was a newlywed, and a deal was made without having to pay a realtor fee. The process of a bigger home search began. God is amazing.

Engineering work was my first desire, but until an opening in that department appeared, I was working as an electrician. Occasionally, engineers would build equipment and install them in my workplace. I would assist and then help maintain the equipment after they left. Although I did not engineer the processes, I was involved in the details like drafting, troubleshooting, and more.

Then came another twist. The amount of work was much lower than the number of electricians available. The company began to cut back on hours. Four-day workweeks were initiated with loss of pay. Then came an opportunity. The company needed technicians to service equipment sold to outside industries. The job meant relocating, which was not taken lightly by my wife. The raise in pay helped to calm the storms in the household. The company guaranteed the sale of our home, would pay for closing costs, and cover all costs to move. In addition my wife and I would travel to house hunt under company expense. We landed in Pittsburgh, Pennsylvania.

Leaving family and friends was hard on Dottie, but she was a trooper. It took less than six months to learn that the job would not be as rewarding as I hoped. Diving into the electronics was replaced with replacing failed components. Engineering was minimal. We were not allowed to repair a failed component like my job in the Air Force required. Dottie was delighted when I contacted my previous boss to see if I would have a job waiting when I came home, and he said yes. Even better, was that the work required overtime, so income would not be an issue. The four-day workweek was lifted. My old boss matched the raise I received and we were homeward bound.

Although the company paid the costs before, this move would be out of pocket. We had to find a three-bedroom home and took a loss on the home in Pittsburgh. Friends and family came to the rescue. The new home was purchased and we didn't seem to feel any pain. God was working out the details.

Within months of starting work again with my former boss, another opportunity arose in the company. The engineering department was looking for technicians in the field to work with engineers. This was a huge step in the right direction.

A NEW COMMITMENT

L ife was great. Raising a family with a loving wife and a career that
seemed to be on the right path. The American dream was being fulfilled.
Our family attended church every Sunday. My deep base voice was
recruited for the choir and the pastor enjoyed my service work. My electrical
background was used to install a complete fire and smoke detector system to
pass local inspection. Still, there was something missing.

Growing up without a mother had a huge impact on my life. Not having
a father around for several years, except for occasional visits, was another
factor. Now I was the father figure with a second child on the way. It was
overwhelming. I desired to be the best that I could be, but doubt crept in. Heavy
workloads and night school classes kept me away from spending time with our
son. Was I acting like my dad by not being there during those formative years?
Jeffrey was about the same age as I was when the first foster home began.

Then a Billy Graham crusade was being televised and it sparked my
interest. I listened to several speakers prior to the message and was captivated.
The message was clear. I needed to turn my life over to a loving Savior and
let Him direct my paths. It wasn't as if I was on the wrong pathway, but the
responsibilities of fatherhood weighed heavily on me. I kneeled down and
made that commitment. Perhaps, I expected a sudden relief or vision to occur,

but that didn't happen. I began to read my Bible daily and pray. One prayer, in particular, was on my heart and lips each morning, namely, "Lord, if something were to happen to me, I pray that you will watch over my family."

That was my way of dealing with my fears as a father. Failing in that aspect of my life was worse than anything that I could do in my workplace. Perhaps, I received some form of relief each morning when I prayed. Perhaps, I needed to feel better prepared for my work, by trusting God to handle the things that were uncertain. Whatever the reasons, I was faithful in praying that prayer daily for about three years. Then something happened that changed everything.

It was Mother's Day nineteen seventy-seven. I travelled across town to pick up my grandmother. She was going to spend the night with us at our home. When I arrived at her house, the phone rang. It was a call for me from my wife. The words from that call stuck in my memory forever. "Our daughter has been hit by a car. Don't worry." Then, I heard "click." As quickly as the words were uttered, she hung up. My heart raced.

The drive from our home to grandmas usually took about thirty minutes. I think I made the return trip in fifteen. Thoughts raced through my mind; most of them were negative. "What happened? Is Tricia hurt? What did my wife mean by 'Don't worry?'" How could I not worry? Needless to say, I was a wreck when I arrived at my home. Dottie's car was not there. I rushed into the house to see if she left a message and found none. I began calling the closest hospital to see if there was admittance under the name of Tricia McIntyre. There was no report. I then called the pediatrician's office. Once again, the answer was negative. I left messages for my wife to return my call. Panic was an understatement.

Finally, a few minutes later, the phone rang. It seemed more like hours. When I answered, immediately, I heard Tricia's voice in the background. I don't remember what she was saying, but it was distinctive, and no doubt it was her voice. Relief flowed through my veins and worries left in a flash. Dottie said that Tricia had a few minor scrapes but otherwise okay. That was the best message that I could receive at that moment in time.

I learned that our neighbor was backing out of his garage when he felt something and immediately stopped his car. His wife yelled to him to stop the car and don't move. They had out of town guests staying with them and their vehicle was parked on the grass near the driveway and towards our house. Tricia was not yet three years of age when she wandered behind the parked car. The neighbor's wife ran out of the house and found Tricia lying down behind the back tire of their car. She was blackened from the car, scared, but otherwise all right.

When I heard about these events, I went to visit the neighbors. They were overjoyed to learn that Tricia was doing well and relieved. They began to share in more detail what happened. I listened intently. The guest car was full-sized and Tricia was several inches shorter. The neighbor's car was mid-sized. Still, the driver would not have easily seen her. Something caused him to hit the brakes. The bruises on her body were not significant to believe that she caused a "thud," as the neighbor said he felt. I believe that it was one of those miraculous interventions by God.

I went into their house to look out the kitchen window, where his wife told her husband to stop the car. That was even more convincing, that God had intervened. There was no way for her to see my daughter's tiny body through the rear quarter panel of their car. Something told her to yell out those words, "Stop the car and don't move." Something told her to look behind that section of their car. They were believers as well, so I am sure God's voice echoed in her mind.

That day was a defining moment in my life. I had been praying for God to watch over my family and he let me know that he was doing just that in a powerful way. My morning prayers took a new turn. I looked back on that day with one thought; "Was I doing vain repetition, when I prayed." That was something that I was taught, namely, to avoid vain repetition. Some denominations repeat phrases in every service and that would make me cringe. Was God trying to get my attention as if to say, "Enough already?" From that day on I uttered prayers, as I felt led. If someone had a need, I would lift it up immediately. The term "popcorn prayer" described it best, where the need was presented quickly and then business as usual. God had my back to be sure.

Still, some things troubled me about the events that took place after the phone call at grandmas. Why did it take so long for my wife to respond from the doctor's office? She was not there when I first called and the drive there was much quicker than I made from grandma's house. I would have jumped in the car immediately with our daughter after hanging up. Then I learned the reason why. When Dottie said, "Don't worry," it meant that Tricia was not seriously hurt, at least as far as she was concerned. The problem was that Tricia was covered with grime from the car. She couldn't be taken to the doctor's office looking like that and didn't need emergency service. Cleaning her up and redressing her took priority, at least in Dottie's mind. That would never have crossed my mind if the situation was reversed and I was there instead of my wife. Tricia's welfare would have taken the highest priority. I may have grabbed a change of clothes, but the time to clean her would have to wait. Nevertheless, I laughed. Now I knew the rest of the story.

A New Career

Working with engineers was like a dream come true. My anticipation was filled with anxiety. I had placed them on pedestals. They had at least four years of college preparation and I was still taking evening courses towards a degree. I felt that I had to work hard to get up to their level. My perceptions were wrong and needed to be corrected. God was working on every aspect of my life.

A department head interviewed me with sixty-five engineers under him. He made it a point to tell me that I was not called up because of my electrical or electronic experience. That shocked me. When I was first placed in the technician program that took me to Pittsburgh, I was placed in a four-week training schedule. The first two were spent in a classroom in the company, where I found myself feverishly taking notes, as components of the equipment were discussed and displayed. I think I filled an inch thick notebook. The next two weeks were spent with hands on in the building where the equipment was quality tested.

After the last two weeks were completed I threw my notes away. I wrote a letter to the head of the training program to discuss issues that would improve the process. The people hired from outside the company first worked on the equipment and then took the classes. It explained why I seemed to be the only one taking notes in class. Employees, who were transferred in, did not have the hands-on experience. I hoped to level the playing field by allowing employees to follow the same course.

The letter made it to my work records and the department head read it. His words to me went something like this: "You are here because of the letter you wrote. You saw a need. You offered a solution and did it without any negative responses. Then you sent it to the right place. That's the kind of person we need in this department. How soon can you start?" I remember wondering why the trip to Pittsburgh did not work out. This interview gave me closure. I was about to embark on a career in the field that I desired. Often we travel down different paths and come to crossroads. The one direction may look like the right one, but God sees the bigger picture. The letter displayed a character trait that opened the doors for the future, when I may have had to wait until completing my degree. I may have written the letter, but God had it in his plan all along.

I was now the new kid on the block surrounded by seasoned engineers. I was overwhelmed. The department head assigned four electrical engineers as lead men over fifteen others. I was assigned to one of these men. I was impressed by the organization plan. The four lead men reported to the department head. By the time my career was over, ten was the limit of workers that a department head could handle. Yet, my group worked together wonderfully with now sixty-six.

The first few weeks were spent learning engineering concepts like drafting, testing, writing specifications, and more. I was eager to learn anything and everything. Then the opportunity came for me to perform engineering tasks. My lead man began giving me small tasks to complete, believing that each would keep me busy for several weeks. He was surprised when I would return with a solution or asked for another assignment days later. My field experience provided a wealth of resources to find what I needed to complete tasks. The company had hundreds of buildings and I transferred every six months within the apprenticeship to many of them. Some were highly technical, with testing labs.

One site, in particular, was special. Bud was my leader. He recognized my potential and singled me out for the most challenging tasks. When engineering came to the buildings under his control, I was told to work with them. I was given wiring schematics to follow. I built and wired cabinets, learned new electronic devices, tested the final products, and completed the installations. When the equipment broke down, I was the lead troubleshooter prior to calling the engineer in charge. That experience allowed me to accomplish engineering tasks quickly. My journey seemed to have the things in place for success. God had prepared me well.

Working as a technician had additional benefits. I was on salary but could receive overtime pay for extra hours. That was not the case for engineers, who were on salary only. The company had a suggestion program, which could pay up to fifty thousand dollars for approval, based on company savings. I earned several awards. One was over fifteen thousand dollars. My department limited the award as being part of my job, but the savings was applied to using my solution on unrelated equipment. That changed everything. Shortly afterwards, I was elevated to full engineer status without completing a four-year degree. It was a way to disqualify me for future suggestion awards, but new doors were about to open. God was wonderfully directing my paths.

The last twenty years of my career were spent working as an engineer. I was responsible for five control patents for the company. Later, I learned that my biological mother worked as a scientist in the company and had a patent recorded as well. That was special to know. My journey led me through the complete path from electrical apprentice to electrician, technician and engineer. That controlled my approach to engineering tasks dramatically different from many of my peers. God was in the details.

I was like a kid in a candy store with each new engineering assignment. My main desire was to leave each design with the tools needed to keep the solutions running smoothly. That involved built-in diagnostics for local support people to use for troubleshooting without the need to call engineering. Documentation was written for service people through engineers with a heavy focus on training. The only calls I would get years after an installation involved training for new people. That meant that I could be that kid in the candy store and design new processes without being tied heavily to the old ones. God is an amazing engineer. Just look at His creation.

I called myself the "bottom up" engineer. Most engineers would come directly out of college without a lot of hands-on experience. They focused on the solution and not as much on how to get there. I tended to design from the bottom much like building a house. First, it would need a strong foundation, then walls, roof, etc. Complicated automation can be broken down into small building blocks as well, still keeping the end goal in mind.

This was a lesson that I could pass on to my engineering team players. On one occasion, one young engineer was feverishly trying to complete a project in my building. The equipment she designed was to be delivered to another building within the company. A maintenance person from that building had been working with her on site and the project was six months late. My manager asked me to support the engineer, whom I will call Sue.

Sue was very intelligent. Her training was well beyond mine as far as software was concerned, but she needed to understand the "bottom up" design process. Being frustrated, she was willing to accept my help. The team gathered on a Monday morning to discuss the project. The function of each section of the equipment was described in detail. As Sue completed a section, I stopped her to ask "What if?" questions. They were designed to help her understand the need to build in diagnostics when an event failed. This intrigued the maintenance man. I then asked if it would be beneficial to include a displayed message to describe the cause of a failure. She agreed that would be good, but she was pressed for time.

Then I asked her, if by engineering these things in could bring the equipment up quicker, would you consider it? She agreed. The result was the equipment was shipped that Friday. In less than a week she saw firsthand the benefit of "bottom up" engineering. My career path had a purpose to be sure. The added benefit came later, when the maintenance man delivered the equipment to his boss. He told him that the reason for the delay was to build in diagnostics to help service the equipment in the future. Sue was off the hook with the customer. God used my training in a wonderful way to help and encourage a coworker. I'm sure it was his plan all along.

The perceptions that I had when first entering the engineering department were unrealistic. Placing people on pedestals may seem right, but also counterproductive. Throughout my career, I would solicit input from anyone involved with an engineering task. That includes operators, management, maintenance personnel, and others. Their ideas and suggestions were important to achieve the best solutions. Sue may have learned that, but God was the originator.

The Bible speaks about this when referring to the human body, which is an amazing engineering marvel.

1 Corinthians 12: 14 – 26 (NIV)
"The body is a unit, though it is made up of many parts; and though all its parts are many, they form one body. So it is with Christ.

For we were all baptized by one Sprit into one body – whether Jews or Greeks, slave or free – and were all given one Spirit to drink.

Now the body is not made up of one part but of many.

If the foot should say, "Because I am not the hand, I do not belong to the body," it would for that reason cease to be part of the body.

And if the ear should say, Because I am not an eye, I do not belong to the body," it would not for that reason cease to be part of the boy.

If the whole body were an eye, where would the sense of hearing be?

But in fact God has arranged the parts of the body, every one of them. Just as he wanted them to be.

If they were all one part, where would the body be?

As it is, there are many parts, but one body.

The eye cannot say to the hand, "I don't need you!" And the head cannot say to the feet, "I don't need you!"

On the contrary, those parts of the body that seem to be the weaker are indispensable,

and the parts that we think are less honorable we treat with special honor. And the parts that are unpresentable are treated with special modesty,

while our presentable parts need no special treatment. But God has combined the members of the body and has given greater honor to the parts that lacked it.

So that there should be no divisioning the body, but that its parts should have equal concern for each other.

If one part suffers, every part suffers with it; If one part is honored, every part rejoices with it."

Although this was a parallel to God's plan for believers to work together, it can be applied to the engineering process. Each part of a process is important and performs the specific designed function. Sue needed to learn how to apply new techniques that were not taught in her college program.

There was some reluctance on Sue's part when I was brought in to assist her. The engineers, that she was close to, had warned her about me. Since my projects were on time and successful, jealousy seemed to rear its ugly head in her division and I had been placed on a blacklist of some sort. After learning my methodology for bringing projects online, Sue became a believer and squelched the rumors about me. She even asked for my support on future projects, eager to learn. God used me to help Sue. Competition between us was changed to complementation. I did not know that there was dissension between us prior to assisting her, based on her peers. Yet, God knew and provided closure.

Later, I read an article in an engineering publication. It stated that companies were hiring college graduates who could not perform engineering tasks quickly. They were addressing colleges to put "hands-on" activities in their curriculums. As I read it, I thought of Sue. I hoped that a bottom-up approach is included as well. I travelled a road after high school that taught me far more than I could have ever imagined. God was travelling with me.

A NEW CHALLENGE

Competitors caused the company to streamline its business. This meant downsizing. Before a series of layoffs would be initiated, early retirement offerings were made. With thirty-two years seniority and only fifty years of age, I qualified. I retired and started my own controls company. Part of the severance package included two weeks' vacation pay for each year of service up to twenty-six years. That meant a year's pay, which I could extend for two years at half pay. That enabled me to launch my business. My wife and I were now "empty-nesters." Dottie handled the finances so well that we were nearly debt free, despite nine years of college support for our kids. Once again, God had the details worked out.

My business began to grow. One company used me to launch their business as an engineer in particular, consuming the heaviest load. An electrician that worked with me on my first patent solution also took the retirement. I introduced him to the company and he was hired. After several successes, they decided to hire their own engineer and my business took a hit. Prior to that, my father had a stroke in Florida and was placed in a nursing home. I felt called to spend time with him, but kept trying to build my business, I was too young to actually retire. God had other plans

The loss of work from that company was a defining moment. The urge to be with my dad grew stronger. The nursing home was in Cocoa Beach, Florida, about forty-five minutes from Orlando. A local distributor, that I had business dealings with as an engineer, opened a division in Orlando. The owner's son was the manager. He tried to get me to come down after retirement to work for him on a line of control systems, which I had used in the past. The loss of revenue in my business and the possibility of work in Orlando provided the push that I needed to honor the call to be with dad. God closed one door to open another.

I packed up my two-door Honda Accord and made the trip. That was a hard decision for me and even harder for Dottie. Our daughter, Tricia, was about to give birth to our first grandchild, so we agreed to allow Dottie to remain. The half pay we were receiving from the company could support her there, while my income would come from the new position. My new boss could not afford to match my old salary, but it was enough to support a one-bedroom apartment rental and expenses. I did not know how long this journey would last as dad was well into his eighties. My goal was to spend as much time with him as I could, while desiring to lead him back to the Lord, which he abandoned after losing our mother. That story will be told later.

The new position was going well. My experience was paying dividends with new customers. My boss was pleased. Weekends were spent with dad. That involved bungee-cording his wheelchair in the trunk and lifting him down into the front seat of that accord. His left side was weak, but somehow we managed. Off we would go for breakfast or lunch. The nursing home was dreary and dad looked forward to getting out. His room was small and filled with stamp collecting books, which he used to collect. Now, stamps were being sent to him regularly from a subscription supplier. He knew that he did something with the stamps, but could not remember what that was. The supplier was called to stop the subscription and they reported that he was their best customer.

Our trips away from the home often involved fishing piers. He enjoyed those times, but I am not sure he could hold a fishing rod anymore. His mind was showing signs of dementia as well. On one occasion, he desired to go find his new car to retrieve the lottery winnings from the back seat. I knew that was untrue, but still drove to places that he directed to find it. After a full day, we returned to the home without success. Then he would say that I didn't believe him about the money. He said that he wanted to use some of it to purchase a larger boat for his older son. I would counter by letting him know that if I did not believe him, why would I spend a whole day searching. He seemed ok with that answer.

The next week I arrived with the words from dad's mouth blasting me for not being there on Tuesday. Somehow, he believed that I would come and take him out again to find the money. I knew how to handle him without conflict. I simply turned away and said, "That's okay, dad. I will come back again when you are not so upset." Without hesitation, he sighed, "Did I tell you how great it is for me to see you?" The tension in the room was gone and off we went again in that two-door Accord. I remember thinking that I should try to find a used van that would make loading a wheelchair easier. Dad could also get into it with less stress. God knew my thoughts.

The following Monday left me speechless. I was sitting in my office in Orlando, when I received a call. A large company desired to meet with me to discuss a job opportunity. They were given my name from an unknown source as a candidate to represent them over the entire state of Florida. I agreed to meet them near the airport. During that meeting two men introduced themselves and the company they represented. One was a salesman named Bill who lived in Orlando. I told them that I had used their competitor's products but was unfamiliar with theirs. They told me that they would train me. Then they asked what salary it would take to hire me. I gave them my final salary earned in my first company, which was considerably higher than what I was earning. Without hesitation, they agreed. Then came the clincher. They said that I would be responsible for statewide travel and would normally get a full-sized vehicle. Instead of a car they asked if I would prefer a van. Wow! God knew my thoughts and came through in a huge way. I thought about a high mileage used van to keep the costs to a minimum. Now I was offered a brand new one with all expenses covered. How great is that.

I contacted my boss to explain the situation before making the decision, although I was sure it was a go. He explained that everything was great. The company he represented, that I was working with, desired to force him to take on a multimillion-dollar inventory. My job offer removed a big dilemma. If he did not take on the inventory then that company would pull out and my job would be eliminated. If he took on the inventory, sales would have to greatly increase to cover the costs. He gave me his blessing and the job was mine. Once again, god saw the bigger picture.

A New Direction

B ill became my salesman and encourager. Learning the systems was painless and he gave me the time and help that I needed. Each time that I learned an aspect of the training, I captured it in writing, which could be used for potential customers. Bill knew that I enjoyed playing a round of golf as well, but that was an expense that I could not afford before. Customers who also enjoyed the game were introduced to me as well as some great golf courses.

On one occasion, Bill asked me to go to a customer site and provide a program solution. I think he thought it would be an all-day event as he was surprised when I called two hours later asking for another assignment. The solution was easy, based on my experience. I remember Bill saying, "Do you have your golf clubs with you?" I responded affirmatively. He said, "Go play." Bill knew that I had been working long hours learning new programs, travelling, and introducing myself to customers. That was his way of telling me to take a break. It was a pat on the back. Perhaps, it was God's way of giving me rest as well.

The new income also meant that I should consider another opportunity, namely, purchasing a house. Paying rent on a single bedroom apartment on the other side of town from where Bill lived seemed wasteful. Our home in New York was paid for, so Dottie's expenses were minimal. When she would fly down to visit, my Accord would be available, even if I were travelling across the state. I found a two-year-old home about three miles from where Bill lived. The owner was a single lady who was engaged to the neighbor next door. I made an offer below asking price and was surprised when it was accepted. Other offers were higher, but she took mine due to less contingencies. Dottie loved the house as it backed up to a protected nature environment. Visits were like vacations and only about a three-hour drive from her best friend, David's wife, Jan. It seemed as though God had that worked out as well.

Weekends were still spent with my dad. On one occasion, my daughter, Tricia, flew down with our grandson, Bryce, as well. Dottie, Tricia, Bryce and I took the van to visit dad. He held his great grandson up with delight. Somehow, he had enough strength to do that. Dad blurted, "He's perfect." The smile on his face was a huge improvement from previous visits.

One Sunday my pastor asked if I had ever been baptized. I replied, "No, but I desired to be." That afternoon was scheduled, so my visit to dad would be cut short. As usual, after the morning service, I drove to see dad. After loading his wheelchair, I removed the large print Bible that was in it and placed it on my dad's lap in the front seat. We drove to a restaurant for lunch, but this time I let him know that I could not stay long afterwards due to my baptism.

Little did I know that those words would trigger the response that I had long awaited from dad. Week after week, my brother and I would visit him and share the salvation message. By this time my source of pleasure involved getting him to laugh at some point in the visit. After the meal we went to the van. As usual, the wheelchair was loaded, dad was helped into the front passenger seat and then I got in. The Bible had slid to the side so I placed it on his lap. Then I said, "Are you reading it, dad?" "I try," was his response. Then I asked if there was something that he did not understand. His words struck my heart with unbelievable joy. "All I know is I want to go to Heaven, because I think that is where my sons are going to be."

When I asked if he knew how to get to Heaven, he responded, "No," despite all of the efforts my brother and I made. There was something about being baptized that triggered such a response. Perhaps, my mother had been baptized or discussed it. Whatever it was, dad was ready to make the decision to accept Christ and receive forgiveness for his sins. When I mentioned that we are all sinners, he blurted, "I haven't done anything wrong." "Oh, really," I responded. "Have you ever held a grudge?" He agreed that he did. "Have you ever been angry?" Once again he affirmed.

After a few more similar questions, I asked him to consider that the creator of the universe was looking down into this van and looking for people to bring into his perfect place called Heaven. "Would He select you, dad?" After answering my previous questions, dad hung his head and said. "No." Then I reassured him that was not true. With some leading, dad prayed three separate prayers. He admitted being a sinner and sought forgiveness. Then he asked the Lord to save him. Finally, he accepted Christ as his Lord and Savior. The first question that I asked dad afterwards was, "Whom do you expect to see in Heaven?" He responded, "Your mother." God planned for this day, the events of dad's stroke, and every detail.

I learned that my mother was Jewish and, before she died, accepted Christ in a Baptist church in upstate New York. Her passing left dad with a void and doubt of God's existence. Stamp collecting, bridge playing, reading, crossword puzzles, and so much more, replaced his spiritual journey. He had come full circle. The stroke left him without food or water in his apartment for three days until his superintendent found him, led by the call of a bridge player. Dad kept his commitments, so missing two consecutive dates was suspect. God was surely with him during those days of being subconscious.

As I drove back to the baptism site, I began calling family members. Dottie was first on my mind. This was the very purpose for my trip to Florida and now it was fulfilled. The tears ran down my face as I tried to get the words out. Dottie felt my joy without words. Then I called David with a similar response. The excitement caused me to miss my turn on the road, but I made the baptismal site on time. During our conversation about baptism, my pastor passed on one piece of information that suddenly came to the forefront. Although baptism is not what saves us, my pastor felt that God withholds a storehouse of blessings until afterwards. Upon arrival to the site, I shouted something to the effect that the floodgates were opened and my dad received salvation today. I shared with my pastor that in this case blessings were poured out before my baptism. I have a certificate of baptism with the same date along with that date entered in my dad's large print Bible. Dad was eighty-nine. God's message was clear. As long as we have breath, salvation is near.

Three weeks later I was overwhelmed with the thought, "Did dad really know what he did?" His mind was certainly warped with delusional thoughts about winning the lottery and not understanding how to view stamps. It seemed as though the stroke took away any hope of comprehension. At least that was what I was thinking and feeling. I asked God for a sign. The following day I went to be with dad. It was Saturday. When I opened his sign-out book I saw that my brother had driven up the day before. Usually, I call him after each weekend's visit to update him on dad's condition, but he did not call me after his visit. On the return home, I called to ask him why. He said that he had the day off and decided to make the three-hour drive to spend time with dad.

Then he said that he took dad to the local pier and, while driving back, something strange happened. I was intrigued. "What happened?" Dad started singing. All through our life we never heard dad sing. He was always quick witted and two-word sentences were considered long. So, to hear him sing would have been amazing. Was this God's answer to my prayer? Before I could respond, my brother continued, "It was not that he was singing that was so strange, but rather what he was singing." Now my interest had peaked. "What was he singing?" I asked. "He sang, 'When the Role is Called Up Yonder, I'll Be There.'"

I'm sure that hymn was from his mother. Perhaps, it was with him in the bunkers in Africa and Normandy during WWII. Regardless, it was the answer that I longed for to my prayer. God is in that business of answering prayer for sure.

Dad had moved to Florida over twenty years earlier. During that time, David witnessed to him on each visit. The seeds were planted, but until dad's stroke, the ground was not fertile. God knew how to prepare the soil. Some do the planting. Others water. God did the harvesting.

The Memorial Celebration

D ad did not make it to his ninetieth birthday. David called me from South Florida on his way up to make preparations. During the prior weeks, we would visit dad to try to get him baptized, but he was too weak. Knowing that his suffering was over and the assurance that Heaven was waiting with open arms, made the news more bearable. I could hear the tears in my brother's voice while he shared his feelings. He was listening to a Christian song on the radio with the words, "If You Can See Me Now." It was a song of joy about what Heaven must be like and spoke directly to his heart. God heard David's prayer and provided relief.

Dad was provided a veteran's funeral. I still have the flag that was presented. There were very few attendees, mostly immediate family. When my stepmother passed away, funeral expenses were made to also handle dad's passing, except for the crypt opening and closing costs. Dad made these details easier to deal with despite a meager income. I think he did not want to be a burden in any way to his boys.

My brother and I led the celebration; at least that is what we desired it to be. I began by having the hymn, "When the Roll is Called Up Yonder," played. Dad's salvation and confirmation was presented. David had his choice played,

"If You Can See Me Now," prior to speaking. The message of salvation was clear. The beauty of Heaven awaits all who place their trust in the Lord. Dad did that and it was a time to celebrate his life.

At the end of the service, two people came forward. They were not family. One was dad's apartment superintendent. The other was the woman who played the music. David spoke to the superintendent, who said something like, "I have been attending church most of my life. I have never heard words like that." He was referring to David's scriptural readings and applications. He was also Catholic. David opened the Bible to him to show the passages. The man said that he had a Bible but never read it. The only time the words were presented to him was from the pulpit in church. Perhaps, afterwards, he would open the Bible and begin a new experience. God only knows.

The lady spoke to me with the words, "I have been doing this for nine years and I have never been moved so much in a service before." Wow! It appears as though we succeeded in uplifting the event, at least for her. I remember lifting my eyes to the sky as if I was talking directly to dad with the words, "In your passing you have already touched two lives here on earth." I could see that she was deeply moved by the tears still in her eyes. She affirmed that they were not tears of sadness. God had moved through that time as well.

What a joy to serve the Lord. My time to go to Florida was well spent, but now I had a new decision to make. "Do I continue to work or return to New York? I enjoyed my job and I'm sure Dottie understood that. I also enjoyed not having to shovel snow in the winter and could play golf year-round. Still, our children were up north with their families. Dottie told me that she did not want me to stop working. I was too young to retire and not old enough for social security. Maintaining two houses was a burden, especially, when I was not there to make any repairs. My hope was to find some middle ground and unite with one house. God knew that was on my heart as well.

A New Opportunity

L ife does not stand still. Decisions have to be made constantly. Dad was gone and my weekend visits along with it. One advantage of living in Florida was that I was close to my brother. The wives were best friends before we met, so Dottie may have had another reason for me to keep working. She could fly down and spend more time with her friend while I travelled the state. The additional income from my first retirement had run out, but my income could still support both places.

The technical writings that I made while learning software in the company reached the training department in Atlanta, Georgia. I was called up there to speak to the head of that department about a year later. I was presented a training manual for a new class to review. Then I was asked what I thought about it. I responded that it looked good. The response I heard astounded me. "It should. It is your work." I was informed that the dozens of short "How to" writings opened up a new door of opportunity for the company. For some time customers would sign up for traditional four and one-half day classes on specific subjects. Many had asked for customized classes that would fill the same time period, but cover multiple needed subjects.

The department head asked if I would like to work for him in Atlanta when a position opened up. His authorization for trainers was full, but when retirement or transfer freed up a slot, I would be contacted. That meant that I would also have to be replaced by someone else in Florida. God knew the timing for both things to happen as well.

I was at home reviewing my emails, when I received one from my daughter. Tricia said that her husband, Adam, desired to move out of state to get a job working in his field and get medical insurance. Tricia was a special education teacher with those benefits and desired to be a stay-at-home mom. A company near Atlanta was interested in hiring Adam. I read that and tears came down almost immediately. They did not know that I was in the process of accepting a position there. Adam's training was in horticulture. New York State had a short growing season, so the likelihood of securing a job there with those benefits looked highly unlikely.

In the spring of two thousand four, Dottie joined Tricia and Adam to house hunt in Georgia. We were also grandparents to Kelly, Tricia and Adam's second child. Little did I know that Dottie also desired to move close to our daughter's new home. An opening in the training department would make that a reality. A house was located and things began to happen. Tricia and Adam closed on their home in New York, a truck and car caravan made the journey towards Atlanta. After they were settled, the news of my job change became excitement to Dottie. She went to visit Tricia and began a house hunting time for us. Sight unseen, I bought the home in Florida. This time she would make the selection and I would approve. God led the way again.

The person selected to replace me in Florida also had a good reason. His wife worked as a professor at the college in Gainesville, Florida. Since the job did not require a specific location, they could remain in their house. He would travel the state of Florida, instead of the many other states that he worked on call. That freed him up for more family time. Once again, God was in control.

Then came the process of selling our homes. New York State had much longer closing schedules than Florida. Three hurricanes came through Atlanta that year, causing damage to homes. I lost a few shingles and was able to make the repairs quickly, without taking the house off the market. By the end of the summer, many potential buyers flooded the market, but with far fewer houses to view. The value of our home was considerably higher and multiple offers came in at asking price. The large increase in equity made a substantial down payment on the house in Georgia, making the sale of the New York property less necessary. By the end of the year we were relocated in Georgia. The house in New York was closed at the beginning of the next year.

Everything looked like a storybook ending. I was still working, but with far less travel. We had one home and were together close to our daughter. The five years spent away from my wife was now all worth it and shoveling snow was now a memory. Life was wonderful, or so it seemed. God was not through with us.

A New Obstacle

dam began working at the nursery, while Tricia stayed home. She homeschooled Bryce and enjoyed it. The income was not the best, but parents were there to help in a pinch. I drove to work about twenty-five miles each way. The trip was faster in the morning as I would leave before traffic was bad. Classes ended, however, when the traffic began to be congested. A forty-minute ride in the morning would take an hour and a half for the return trip. Still, I enjoyed the work and looked forward to being with my wife afterwards.

After spending Easter with our daughter in two thousand five, Dottie felt discomfort on her side. At first, she thought it came from eating too much, but when it continued into the following week, she made an appointment with the doctor. I was conducting a training seminar in Atlanta, when my wife called. She had been to see the doctor, who sent her over to the nearby hospital for further tests. A ten-centimeter mass was found on her liver and biopsies determined that it was cancer. The news took me by surprise and my boss relieved me from all training responsibilities. I needed to be by Dottie's side.

I was about an hour from home. That made negative thoughts pass through my head like a whirlwind. "How can this be? We finally get together under one roof and this happens?" The list goes on. All I knew was that I needed to be with her. We went to an oncologist to discuss her treatment and options. One of my questions to him involved how long the disease had been growing. The best guess he could share was about five years, based on where it had spread. That hit me hard. About that time was when I left for Florida. Could my decision caused my wife to have cancer? Although she tried to dismiss that thought, it remained for some time.

Then we learned that the cancer had spread into her lungs and back. That required a series of radiation treatments on her back as step one. That was successful and offered momentary relief for both of us. Then a series of chemo treatments were prescribed. The problem the oncologist had was finding where the cancer started. That would give him the best chemo options to pursue. Eventually, it was titled, "unknown primary." The first chemo treatment lasted about six weeks. Dottie handled it well, but was very weak. The results showed some success, but more was needed.

A second series of about the same length was implemented after Dottie regained her strength and her body could handle it. She would joke about the fluids as if she was off to get her drink. She knew the Lord and trusted him completely. No matter what she would have to endure, her faith was sufficient. She knew she could endure all things through Christ. Her favorite verse came from Philippians.

Phil. 4:13 (NIV)
"I can do everything through him who gives me strength."

She was a saint and was more concerned about others than herself. You would hear only positives from her. During the lulls between treatments she enjoyed walking with family and friends. One of those was a lady named Brenda, whom she met while walking in a park with Tricia. When Tricia was unavailable to walk, Brenda was willing. Dottie would also meet Brenda for lunch or go shopping. I would hear the name passed in conversation, but did not meet her until later. Brenda was devout and shared Dottie's belief and interests.

Dottie first met Brenda before learning of her cancer. God had provided a close and needed friend.

Brenda and her husband returned from a vacation in San Francisco, when illness struck. Her husband had cancer and it was more advanced. Within a few months he was in Heaven. The roles had reversed. Dottie was now Brenda's comforter. "Was God in control? Was Dottie's cancer necessary, so that she could help Brenda in her darkest hour?" The questions flowed.

Another chemo treatment was introduced for Dottie, that showed some promise, but the effect was short lived. After all options were tried, the oncologist suggested a new option. A company in Houston, Texas, introduced a new gene therapy approach. That involved out-of-pocket costs, travel expenses, and time. We made the trip and began the preparation. Dottie was told to take a pill for six days. The first day required one dose. The second day she would take two, and etc.

On the first day, Dottie felt fine so she dropped me off at a local coffee house and drove around the city. She picked me up that evening for dinner. The next day she felt weak and stayed in the motel. On the third day, she felt so bad that I rushed her to the clinic where the tests were being performed. They immediately rushed her to the nearby hospital. She had developed pneumonia. Everything took a turn for the worse, as her vital signs were extremely poor. I bought a ticket for our son, Jeffery, to fly down and called Tricia, who made the trip by car. If their mother was going to be with Jesus, they needed to pay last respects. God had other plans.

Within a few days, Dottie's vitals improved. We gathered by her side in the hospital, laughed together, and enjoyed family time. Jeff lived in New York State, so having him there was special for everyone, since we didn't see him that often. The next morning, we received a call from Dottie requesting donuts. First, let me share that this was something out of the ordinary. Dottie preached to us about the dangers of fat grams. She walked nearly every day as well to inspire good health habits. Donuts did not make the grade as nutritious, or so we thought.

Since Houston was new to us, we asked if she knew of any donut shops in the area. "Lots of them" she said. "Shipley's, there everywhere." Not only did she know the name, but gave Tricia directions as to where to go. In addition, Dottie specifically requested Boston crème donuts and told Tricia where they were in the donut shop. "How could she know all of this?" was my question. Then I realized that the only time she spent in that city was after she dropped me off at the coffee house. She was on a mission. All that talk about fat grams went out the window. I sure hope they have donuts in Heaven, especially Boston crème.

The hospital was about to release her and further treatment at the clinic was stopped. The trip seemed to be a failure, so whatever happens was in God's hands alone. I drove my car alone back to our home, while Tricia drove with her mom. The cancer was still there, but Dottie had enough strength to live a reasonable life. I continued working during the day, but the company allowed me to work from home as much as possible. Training assignments outside the area were given to other trainers. That was a blessing.

One Saturday morning Tricia received a call from mom. "Do you think the kids would like some donuts? "I'm sure they would" was her reply. Minutes later, Dottie arrived with a dozen donuts, or should I say ten. Two Boston crèmes were missing. Then Bryce, Kelly, Tricia and Dottie enjoyed a few for themselves. When Dottie was preparing to leave, Tricia asked if she would like to take a donut home for dad. She said yes. The next morning at church, Tricia turned to me and asked if I enjoyed the donut. I said, "What donut?" Then Dottie turned to Tricia and said, "It didn't make it." We laughed and still laugh about it today. Anytime we have a Boston crème we acknowledge that it was for her. Anything that would bring pleasure to her was received with open arms, especially donuts.

We had no timetable as to how long Dottie would have left or whether God would miraculously heal her. We lived day by day. On those times when she felt good, she would actively engage in outside activities. Tricia, her kids, and Dottie decided to go bowling near where I worked. I was to join them when I could. Just before I was to leave to meet them, Tricia called with more bad news. I hurried to the bowling alley. Dottie had vomited a lot of blood. I rushed her to the nearest hospital and they rushed her in to emergency. Outside the intensive care room I could see her vitals displayed on a monitor. "How can she be alive?" A normal blood pressure reading might be 120 over 80. Hers was 20 over 10. I called her best friend, Jan, in Florida to tell her the news. Jan was a retired registered nurse and could help me understand those readings. Like me, she felt alarmed.

Within an hour, her blood pressure reached normalcy and she was wheeled back to a holding room. The blood seemed to have stopped. Transfusions were administered. The doctors placed tubes down her esophagus to locate a source of blood leakage. They suspected that her stomach had filled slowly from a cut, but could not locate the source. Around midnight she was released and we went home. At five o'clock that morning the vomiting came back again. An ambulance was called and she was rushed back to the hospital. This time they located the cut at the end of the esophagus and were able to cauterize it. God still had things to accomplish.

JOURNEY HOME

For the next few weeks, Dottie's health waned. She would have her good days, but they were few. Still, she continued to keep her spirits up and was a blessing to all visitors. Jan decided to fly up and stay with us. Her nursing skills were another blessing and it would offer some relief for me. I longed to enjoy a round of golf, but needed to stay by her side continuously. Jan's arrival was truly a godsend. Tricia thought that Jan became a nurse for this very purpose; to be with her best friend during the last days. I agreed. Perhaps, God had that in his plans all along.

It was truly a joy to watch the two of them laugh and share together. On one occasion, Dottie was propped up with pillows while sitting on the couch. She didn't have the strength to stay upright. The pillows failed to hold her up and she began to fall to the side. While falling she yelled, "Whoops." We couldn't help but laugh hysterically, and she laughed with us. Friends and pastors would stop in and her spirits lifted them as well. Brenda was one of them, so I got to meet her for the first time. She was a pleasant lady and I could now put the face with all of Dottie's stories that referred to her.

While all of this was going on, Kelly was scheduled for open-heart surgery. She was born with a leaky valve, which the doctors would correct when she turned five. Just before her operation, Dottie was rushed to the hospital again. Her vital signs were poor and the oncologist met us there. The prognosis was not unexpected. He said that her organs were failing and it would only be a matter of time, perhaps a week or two. At the same time, Kelly was undergoing her surgery. I was torn between being with her and staying with my wife. "Why was this happening at the same time?" That was my message to God.

I remained with Dottie, but longed for a report of the operation. The hospitals were about forty minutes apart by car. It was time to consider hospice at home. I had set up an appointment with one source for three o'clock that afternoon, when Tricia called to update me on the operation. It was a complete success and I could visit no earlier than the next day. Then I told her about the need for hospice. One of her close Christian friends had joined a hospice group in the area where I lived and I felt relief. "Could she come to this hospital before two?" The call was made and Tricia joined us as well.

Everything seemed to be coming together for this decision. Not only would I get hospice help, but also they would be local and my daughter's friend. The hospice lady arrived, whom I will call Joann. Joann handed me her portfolio. I opened it and was awestruck by the words on the top of the page. I showed it to Tricia, who yelled. "Oh my God! That's your book, dad." Joann said, "Are you a writer?" I explained that after my dad passed away, I wrote a book about his life for my family called, "Legacy of Love," which were the words at the top of the page. It was another sign that this was the right choice for the care I would need. We parted ways after agreeing to use her help. Once again, God had other plans.

My three o'clock appointment representative arrived as we were leaving. I told her that her services would not be needed, but kept her information anyway. The next day I received a call from Joann telling me that my insurance would not cover them. I quickly contacted the original representative and signed with them. My mind was racing. "Why did this happen? Everything was great. Why did I meet with Joann?" Then it hit me. I needed to read those words on her folder. God desired for me to publish that work for the world.

I wrote that book about seven years earlier, spiral bound it, and gave it to family and a few friends. My friends, who read it, told me to publish it, but I said it was for family. Many others shared the same comments and got the same responses. Then I began to question other things that were strange, like, "Why did I have to go to Houston?" That was a complete disaster. Then I remembered meeting someone in a coffee shop who was writing a thousand-page novel on the Civil War. I was impressed and struck up a conversation with him. During the conversation, I told him about a book I wrote for my family. After telling him what it was about, he told me that the world needed to read it. Again I denied that I would publish it. He insisted on writing the name of a book on the back of his business card that helped him to find a publisher. I remember putting that card in my wallet and thanked him. I located the card and turned to see the man's name. What I saw was where he was from, Houston, Texas.

Suddenly, things began to make sense. That trip was not about Dottie. It was for me. I only spent one day in that coffee house, but it changed my life. I knew I had to publish that book. God had me on a journey for sure. He was directing my paths.

A Day to Remember

I contacted my boss to let him know that I would retire at the end of the month to spend the remaining time that I had with my wife at home. The month was May and the year was two thousand and seven. I located the book that the author recommended to pursue publication. I purchased it and began to follow the guidelines, but did not find it useful. I realized that the point was not what he wrote on his card, but rather, that I needed to seek publishing.

In the meantime, Jan cared for Dottie and told me to play golf. I needed that break. Dottie's last days were with her family and closest friend. Jan gave me instructions on how to administer morphine if necessary, but I did not have to do that. On June 1, Dottie took a turn for the worse. I called Tricia to hurry over as Jan said she did not have much longer. She died peacefully that day.

June first was my official retirement day. It was also Tricia and Adam's anniversary date. Kelly was born on that day as well. I remember Tricia uttering the words, "Why did she have to leave us on this day?" I had no answer. When Brenda lost her husband, she was blessed with her youngest grandchild. Sometimes, I think that when a loved one passes, another comes to lift our spirits. That may have been the case for Brenda. Perhaps, Kelly being born on the day five years ago was to be my solace. It was and is a day that my family and I will remember. I have much to be thankful for.

Our family conducted two services, one in Georgia and the other back north. We wanted them to be celebrations with family and friends. Most of them were in New York State. Tricia spent the bulk of the preparations. She made a CD with pictures and music as a gift for all guests. It was amazing and an act of love. I think a hundred copies were distributed.

I was comforted by family, but still grieving from the loss. At the end of the service in Georgia, I began to shake uncontrollably. My brother saw me trembling and took me outside for some fresh air. After several minutes the shaking ceased. My emotions took on a visible expression. I may have held things inside for the benefit of others, but the realization of Dottie's passing triggered their release. It was also evidence of how much I loved her.

I received a call from Brenda a few weeks after Dottie's passing. "Hello. I just wanted to say, hey." Those words were so welcoming. My house was no longer a home. The silence was deafening. The TV was turned on just for noise as I began to write a new ending for my book. Her voice was a refreshing break. I may have answered her with "hey," but that was a southern expression. She told me that she knew what I was going through and that I could call her anytime.

I remember calling her with the words, "You have to eat. I have to eat. How 'bout going out to eat together?" Looking back, that sounded crude, but it worked. God had provided a new source of support. Her name was Brenda.

A New Path

I remember thinking about retirement and how I would live. I was a few years away from Social Security, but could live meagerly on some IRA investments. Then I received a call from my workplace manager. He understood why I retired, but wondered if I would consider working as a consultant, I said that I would and a new road was to be travelled. The month of May was my last working month for them, but I used it to write new course materials. I envisioned that it would open new doors of training opportunities for the company. I was always appreciative about how they let me work from home and put my family first over their own needs.

Boy was I surprised when they told me that I would head the new course training. After a few classes, it took off. If I desired, I could work full time travelling to sites across the country. Other instructors needed to be trained to lead the classes to handle the requests. Since I was no longer on salary and the company did not have to pick up healthcare and other costs, my compensation was even better. Two or three classes a month would net more than full time work. Once again God came through.

In two thousand eight, I published "Legacy of Love" through a Christian publisher. I added Dottie's story after my dad's as a second legacy. One of the first non-family readers was a single lady who worked in the company. I trained her to teach one of my classes. Prior to going on the road to lead a class, I stopped by the building where she worked to pick up materials that I would need. I had given her the book two weeks earlier. When I arrived, she saw me and began to hug me with excitement. "What's going on," I remarked. She said that she read my book and then gave it to her ex-husband to read. I was happy to hear that, but then she held up her left hand with a sparkling diamond ring. I knew her for eight years and her last name was hyphenated. So I thought she had been married before. Then she said. "We have remarried." Wow! That was instant affirmation that I needed to publish the book for the world. God planned that all along.

Between work assignments, I used writing as a coping mechanism for the loneliness I felt at home. I began recalling people in my life that had an impact in my life. The first that came to my mind was Molly. I never knew her last name, but met her in the coffee shop that I enjoyed prior to going to work in New York. I would leave home an hour or more before I needed to, so that my family would enjoy hot showers when they awoke. The electric hot water heater would not recover quickly, leaving the third or fourth shower turning cold. The hour difference was my way of helping out. Even after the heater was replaced with a gas one, I continued the habit my entire career.

Molly showed up one morning and ordered a cup of tea. Her demeanor was sad as she sat on the counter stool beside me. I felt the urge to introduce myself. "Excuse me. My name is Dennis. I sense something is wrong with you. Can I help?" To this day I don't know what led me to do that. I was not that bold before. I can only believe that God triggered those words. Molly responded with a barrage of information. Her husband was going blind and about to receive a medical retirement. She was a stay-at-home mom with two boys preparing for college and more. My introduction was like opening a faucet and watching the water come out in force.

At some point, I interrupted her. I began to share a story about my dad. My stepmother began to lose her eyesight after they retired to Florida, which

I shared with her. Then I used the words, "But Molly. My dad didn't look at it like you." Molly seemed to have a moment of reprieve. "How did your dad look at it?" "Dad lost his first wife when I was three. He remarried when I was eight or nine. The only mother I knew helped him through the toughest times. Now he was in a position to help her. He looked at it as an opportunity to give back. It was his way of saying thanks." Those may not have been the exact words, but Molly got the message.

I headed to Florida seventeen years later. I saw Molly regularly for seventeen years. I saw her get a job working the late shift at a nearby hospital. After work she would still come to the coffee shop. I knew her boys graduated from college and her life was good. The owner of the coffee shop asked me when I was heading to Florida. I told her that my last day at her shop would be that Thursday.

Typically, three or four people at a time would be present during my time there, which usually lasted close to an hour. My original workplace was only minutes away. That Thursday, the place was packed. I think there were close to twenty people. They each signed a card and shared their stories with me. Without my awareness, God had been using me to encourage them. I was blown away. Molly was the last to share. "Remember when you first met me?" She asked. I replied affirmatively. I referred to her husband's eyesight, retirement and other details. She said, "You don't know the rest of the story." The tears were pouring down my face from the sharing before, but I asked if she was going to tell me the ending.

"The day we met was also the day that I had an appointment with my doctor. I was under his care for depression. As I entered his office he shouted, 'Molly, what happened to you?' Those words took me by surprise. I thought something was wrong, but I answered, what do you mean?" He said, "You look so upbeat today." "Oh, I just met this wonderful man in a coffee shop. Then I shared the story about your dad with him. Do you know what he told me?" "No, but I hope you will tell me." The tears were still flowing.

"He said, 'you don't need me anymore. Just keep going to that coffee shop.'" Molly had followed her doctor's advice and stopped his care. I was overwhelmed with the thought that she desired to meet me for all those years, even after working a night shift job at the hospital. My pastor told me that I had the gift of encouragement, but until that moment I did not believe it. That was another defining moment for me.

I continued writing short stories as they came to mind. I titled the collection, "Coffee Shop Ministries." I made a few spiral bound copies and gave them to friends. Their comments were positive. Several said that the title should be "Divine Appointments." The book, "Coffee Shop Ministries," was first self-published around two thousand nine. I ordered a hundred books and used them as a ministry. In two thousand twenty, it was formally published with a much-improved cover. If anyone desires to read Molly's story and the others, it is now available online through major carriers.

One of my friends from Florida had a website that began placing one of my coffee shop stories each month on their site. Their hits quadrupled almost immediately. That inspired at least one more story from a viewer. Molly's story caused a retired couple to contact the website desiring to talk to the author. They left their phone number, which my friend passed on to me. I called them and listened to their story. After several phone conversations, despair had been replaced with joy and hope. Their story was added to the collection. God still had work for me to accomplish.

As mentioned in my introduction, my Florida friend contacted me in two thousand eleven to come down. That usually meant a round of golf as he lived on a course. This call had a different purpose. I made the drive and was introduced to a Christian man with a changed life. My friend handed me a small tape recorder and some tapes to record the man's story. As a result, I wrote my first novel titled, "Shackled Yet Free." The only thing that was changed was the ending. I had it self-published so that copies could be obtained for my friend and others.

Two ladies from my local church read the story and told me that they couldn't wait for the next one. I was caught off guard. I did not think of myself as a novelist. Short stories comprised my previous writings, which were based on actual events. These ladies wanted to know what happened to a character in the man's life, which was abandoned. Writing this would mean total fiction. I was living alone, so writing felt good. It gave me something to pass the time. I wrote two more novels as a trilogy. They can be obtained through major carriers as well. The first was titled, "Freedom's Journey." The second was titled, "Free to Serve." Perhaps God provided writing skills as a witnessing tool.

Math and science was my high school forte with English well down the list. The covid epidemic in two thousand twenty ended my technical training career. Writing had taken on a new direction. A movie script was written for "Shackled yet Free," which won first place at an international film festival. Professional readers have reviewed the other novels with rave reviews as well. Two children's books and additional works are being published. God has directed my paths in mighty ways. I pray that His message is proclaimed to the world through these works. I can't wait for where He will lead me next.

A NEW COMPANION

The loss of my wife left a huge hole. I envisioned celebrating a fifty-year anniversary together. My oldest brother has obtained that mark. My younger brother is almost there. Knowing that we have had sustained marriages is another blessing as well, despite a troubled childhood with the loss of our mother. I am sure that we would be found in the minority when it comes to lasting marriages today.

God knew that we needed a lifelong helpmate. Loneliness is a human problem. God first formed man and gave him dominion over the earth.

Genesis 2:18 (KJV)
"And the Lord God said, It is not good that man should be alone; I will make him an help meet for him."

Living alone, after nearly thirty-nine years of marriage, was exactly that, lonely. Each time Brenda would call and say, "Hey," was uplifting. My poor excuse for asking her out for a meal together worked and she accepted.

Nearly fifteen years later we are still best friends and enjoy just being together. The proposition of marrying again has been tried, but it is not a detriment to our relationship. Brenda has completely filled the void in my heart. She has said that I have done that for her as well. Friday nights are still date nights. I still love to open a door for her. My hands-on skills have provided many moments of support. Her skills have helped me as well, perhaps, even more. Our faith keeps us grounded, while our fellowship keeps loneliness away. God has brought us together. I am even sure that Dottie would approve. What a blessing.

As I reflect back, I can see that God had been walking beside me. Why did Dottie have to leave when everything was coming together? That question plagued me and I am sure that it raised its head to so many others who have lost a spouse. We can only see an instantaneous snapshot. God sees the whole picture. Our decisions are based on a few facts in comparison. My relationship with Brenda has opened my eyes on many areas of concern that were present during my marriage.

I would like to reflect on one, a big one. Very early in my marriage, a "brick wall" troubled me. Like many relationships, conflicts will occur. I was not a Christian when I married and Dottie was. Her mother was a Christian, but her father seemed to rebuke the idea. They would have many quarrels, usually ending up with verbal abuse. Dottie witnessed those times and vowed to never do the same when she got married. The first time we faced a conflict was after our honeymoon. The wall went up almost immediately when I spoke. I thought my side wasn't being heard so I would raise my voice. That was the trigger she needed.

Over the years we learned to settle our differences by separating and writing our thoughts down. It seemed like a good plan as tempers would be under control and each of us could read without applying body language. It worked, at least for us. I truly loved her. I never liked to see her upset, which my early reactions to the "brick wall" would cause. Still, part of me desired to have open discussions and end conflicts before going to bed. Often the process of reading thoughts on paper would cover a day or more.

The first time a conflict between Brenda and I came up, I applied what I had learned. I retreated to write down my thoughts. I was fond of her and did not want to cause her to be upset by pushing the issue. To my surprise, I was doing just that by retreating. The process might occur over several days. She said to me, "Why are you treating me like a child?" By not calling her to share my feelings, she felt belittled. She would say something like, "You need to get in my face." She was like a breath of fresh air, as that is what I longed for in my marriage from the beginning.

I believe that God had every part of my being under control. Like Dottie, we make life choices. Many of those may stem from watching our parents. Choices are a normal part of life. My choice to accept Jesus Christ as my savior like she had done was the best one. Her loss opened the doors for me to begin a writing career as part of my witness. Perhaps, that was God's plan all along as well. With each new work, including this one, I ask for His blessing. Let my work be pleasing and honoring to Him.

I am not alone because of Brenda in my earthly walk. None of us are alone with Christ in our hearts. Dottie is with her savior. That much I know is true. I may not know why she left so early, but I am confident that God had a higher call for her.

A Message of Hope

Depression is rampant in this world. Something is missing that causes a person to commit suicide. Money won't fill the void, nor will fame. Some turn to alcohol or drugs, but that only numbs the feelings for a short time. Jesus waits for us to come to him.

Matthew 11:28 – 30 (KJV)

"Come unto me, all ye that labour and are heavy laden and I will give you rest.

Take my yoke upon you and learn of me; for I am meek and lowly in heart: and ye shall find rest unto your souls.

For my yoke is easy, and my burden is light."

These words were written for the human race. We have been given a living soul as recorded in Genesis.

Genesis 2:7 (KJV)

*"And the Lord God formed man of the dust of the ground, and breathed into his nostrils the breath of life; and man became a **living soul.**"*

We have been set apart in creation from everything else. Depression is a disease of our soul. We try to cure it with bodily things that will never work. God desires for us to have abundant life, but without Him, we fall short. His **yoke** is easy and our **burden light**, when we allow Him to come into our very soul and take the lead. A fascinating feature of a yoke is that when two oxen are joined together they perform far more than apart. Single oxen, for example, may pull eight hundred pounds, but together they pull over two thousand. Farmers have learned that principle.

Whatever we are going through in life, we don't have to go through it alone. That is our Creator's promise. We have a special gift reserved for mankind alone, namely, the Holy Spirit. He fills our soul and brings out just the right words to say to someone in pain, like Molly. He encourages others and us, like the patrons in the coffee shop without our awareness. He calms our souls when diversity comes in our paths.

We are all on this journey in life. We can try to travel alone or we can let God lead the way. I have been on a journey that desires the words, "Well done," to meet me at Heaven's gate. Others may be on a journey of destruction. Still there are those who prefer to travel without a roadmap to guide them. We live in a world full of many conveniences, like the GPS systems accessible on our phones. Those work great when we enter the desired destination.

Do you know where life is leading you or are you taking steps one day at a time? Are you working hard to raise a family and not taking time to rest and enjoy them? Is your work enjoyable and fulfilling? These are a few of the questions that may fill our thoughts, but there is one more that needs to be asked. Do you feel that you are alone in your journey?

Looking back on my life is all the evidence that I need to know the answer to that question. God has been with me. God has used me to encourage others while I was unaware. God has protected my family in miraculous ways. He provided a needed van when it was only a passing thought. He directed me to places like Houston, Texas and Pittsburgh, Pennsylvania for my growth. He provided a helpmate for me after the loss of my dear wife. He has been my constant companion. That realization is exciting and wonderful.

It is my prayer that my readers will examine their lives and find joy in knowing that they are not alone. To those who know Jesus, I pray that your journey of life leads others to Him as well. To others going through grief, I pray that you can feel the comforting arms of Jesus embracing you in love. Our earthly voyage is far too short to waste it wandering. Let Jesus lead you. Enjoy His company. Let His love fill your heart.

Romans 5:1 (NIV)

"Therefore, since we have been justified through faith in his promises, we can have peace with God through our Lord Jesus Christ, through whom we have gained access by faith into this grace in which we now stand."

The creator of the universe offers tremendous peace for all who put their faith in Him. It is a peace that goes beyond anything we can imagine. Why would He do this?

John 3:16 (NIV)

"For God loved the world that He gave his one and only Son, that whoever believes in Him shall not perish but have eternal life."

John tells us that it is because of His great love for the world. Anyone who believes can live forever with Him. That is a special invitation for mankind.

Genesis 1:26,27 (NIV)

"Then God said, 'Let us make man in our own image,' in our likeness, and let them rule over the fish of the sea and the birds of the air, over the livestock, over all the earth, and over all the creatures that move along the ground.'"

"So God created man in his own image, in the image of God he created him; male and female he created them."

"Let us" indicates that God had a relationship already. He desired more. We have been created in his "image." What a privilege.

Genesis 2:7 (NIV)
"The Lord God formed the man from the dust of the ground and breathed into his nostrils it the breath of life, and man became a living person."

Only mankind (male and female) has been set apart from all creation as living beings. Life began with the breath of God. God desires a special relationship with us forever.

John 10:10 (NIV)
"The thief comes only to steal and kill and destroy; I have come that they may have life and have it to the full."

In order to have real faith in Him, we are being tested. Satan is on a mission of destruction. He places things in our lives that lead us astray. Money, fame, and other things are not eternal. They are gone when we die. Alcohol and drugs may offer short-term relief from life's setbacks, but real peace lasts forever. Our time on earth is the only thing that allows us to seek God, trust His promises, and accept the gift of his son. We cannot earn our way to heaven. Our only hope is to receive Christ and begin our journey on earth with a personal relationship with God. Then we need to hang on and enjoy the ride.

The Road to Heaven

A s a new father I felt inadequate. Leaning on my heavenly father was the best decision that I ever made. Looking back, I can see that he has been beside me even before I made that choice. Not only that, but he desired to use me to help others find the road to heaven's gate. Writing has been my way to deal with the loss of my wife, but I trust it may be a ministry of service.

Heaven is waiting, but the gates are not open. Jesus is knocking on each heart waiting for our response.

Revelation 4:20 (KJV)
"Behold, I stand at the door, and knock: If any man hear my voice, and open the door, I will come in to him, and he with me."

Our response:

1. Recognize that we are imperfect. We are sinners. Romans 3:23 (KJV) tells us: *"For all have sinned, and come short of the glory of God."*

2. Understand that sin has a price to pay. Romans 6:23 (KJV) lets us know what that is. *"For the wages of sin is death; but the gift of God is eternal life through Jesus Christ our Lord."*

3. Jesus has paid the price. Romans 5:8 (KJV) assure us. *"But God commendeth his love toward us, in that, while we were yet sinners, Christ died for us."*

4. Ask for forgiveness. Pray and admit that you are a sinner.

5. Ask Christ to be your Savior. Romans 10:9, 13 (KJV) provides how. *"That if thou shalt confess with thy mouth the Lord Jesus, and shalt believe in thine heart that God hath raised him from the dead, thou shalt be saved. ...For whoever shalt call upon the name of the Lord shall be saved."*

dennisamcintyre.com

Lightning Source UK Ltd.
Milton Keynes UK
UKHW010645260922
409457UK00001B/91